I HAVE A VOICE
EMPOWERING CHILDREN TO PROTECT THEIR INNOCENCE

I HAVE A VOICE

EMPOWERING CHILDREN TO PROTECT THEIR INNOCENCE

**WRITTEN BY
NENA DAVIS**

**ART BY
JOHN MANN**

**CHIEF CREATIVE DIRECTOR
DAVIS MASON**

**LAYOUTS AND EDITED BY
TREVOR REECE**

**PRODUCED BY
PHIL STAPLETON
STAPLETOONS STUDIOS**

I HAVE A VOICE: EMPOWERING CHILDREN TO PROTECT THEIR INNOCENCE
COPYRIGHT © 2021 NENA DAVIS.
All rights reserved. The story, all names, characters, and incients portrayed in this production are fictitious. No identification with actual persons (living or deceased), places, buildings, and productions is intended or should be inferred.
Printed in the USA.

Whether I feel unsafe or uncomfortable around...
MY FAMILY
MY FRIENDS
MY MENTORS
MY COACHES
MY BABYSITTER
OR ANYONE ELSE

I will use my voice to tell someone to ask for help to keep me safe.
911

"I can wash my own body, my parents taught me how."

"Just a minute..."

"I need my privacy when I am taking a bath, using the bathroom and getting dressed."

"I AM SMART! I AM STRONG! I know the difference between right and wrong!"

Never be afraid to say "I need my privacy!"

SSHHHH... DON'T TELL ANYONE...

No! I will not tell your lies!
No! I will not keep this a secret!
No way! No How!
I am going to tell right now!

DAD

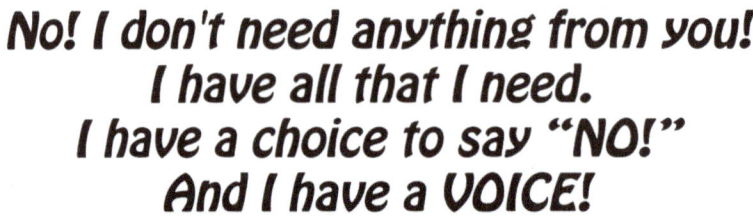

I HAVE A VOICE

EMPOWERING CHILDREN TO PROTECT THEIR INNOCENCE

MEET THE HEROES

DAVIS MASON

Davis Mason is a child actor and the inspiration for our hero, Vixor. Davis is best known for his guest appearance on NBC's Primetime Emmy Award-Winning series, "This Is Us." He is also known for his principal role on ABC's comedy television series, "Abbott Elementary." His hobbies are playing piano, tap and hip-hop dance, swimming, and a multitude of outdoor activities.

VIXOR

When he screams, Vixor's voice can be heard all over the world, but only by the kids he's trying to protect. By tapping the V on his chest, he can shrink or grow giant, letting him go underneath doors or climb up a building wall to help save kids.

JAGGER

He can turn into a jaguar and run really fast. When Jagger roars, his roar can make predators freeze in place while Jagger uses his super speed to save any kids in danger.

COOLEIGH

Cooleigh can freeze people's minds and even read them. This power helps her stop predators from doing bad things before they do them.

SCARLETT

Scarlett can help heal old wounds with her touch. She can help kids deal with feeling uncomfortable and unsafe around anyone.

FLEXOR

Flexor is very flexible and can stretch his arms and his whole body. He can easily grab things or people. He can also shift and blend into any surroundings like a chamaeleon, which helps him watch over and protect kids against predators.

MIKO

Miko has superhuman ears. She can hear when kids are in danger. She also has the power to teleport through portals to help kids in danger and all of her team can use Miko's portal.

ZEALOUS

Zealous can transform into any animal and move through any home or building to save and protect the children. She is very devoted and has a strong passion for helping vulnerable kids.

If you are experiencing any issues related to this topic, you can find more information here:

www.rainn.org
1-800-656-HOPE (4673)

For every book sold, $1 will be donated to organizations dedicated to ending this problem.

www.ihaveavoicebynrd.com

- @ihaveavoice_bynrd
- I Have a Voice by NRD
- Ihaveavoicebynrd
- @ihaveavoicebynrd
- ihaveavoicebynrd@gmail.com
- stapletoonsstudios@gmail.com

I HAVE A VOICE
EMPOWERING CHILDREN TO PROTECT THEIR INNOCENCE

Nena Davis is a professional hairstylist in the TV and Film industry. She was nominated for a Primetime Emmy in 2021 and 2022 for her work on ABC's Black-ish. Her desire to become an author was ignited in 2020 when her son expressed his concerns about speaking to adults when in trouble. Therefore she began developing her book and landed here with her book I have a voice

"I HAVE A VOICE" is her first book.

A MESSAGE FROM THE AUTHOR

"As a single parent who works in the industry, I rely on my village to watch my son, Davis. That has meant taking him to different babysitters and the homes of family and friends. I wanted to make sure that he was fully aware of what unsafe touch is. I did not want him to be afraid of speaking out and saying 'No' if someone tried to touch him inappropriately. I hope this book will be helpful to you, your children, your family and friends. This is a critical and serious problem, that is not always openly spoken about, and continues to affect millions of children every year. This book is my contribution to help children all over the world find their voice."

Your Notes

Your Notes

www.ingramcontent.com/pod-product-compliance
Lightning Source LLC
Chambersburg PA
CBHW061051090426
42740CB00002B/113